The Untroubled Mind

The Untroubled Mind

Herbert J. Hall

DD BOOKS
Publishers for New Generations

This book is an Illustration, although the publisher has made every effort to Illustrate this book but there may still be some grammatical errors in it. If any such thing is found please contact us at the email below.
Every effort has been made to ensure the accuracy of this book's content. However, the publisher assumes no legal liability for errors or omissions. It is not the publisher's intention to offend any reader.

First Published: 2024

Book Name: The Untroubled Mind (Illustrated)
Author: Herbert J. Hall, M.D.

Illustrated by **DD Books**

Price: 250/-
ISBN: 978-93-5957-694-7
Published by **DD BOOKS**
Email: **ddsalesglobal@gmail.com**

Table of Content

Preface

A very wise physician has said that "every illness has two parts—what it is, and what the patient thinks about it." What the patient thinks about it is often more important and more troublesome than the real disease. What the patient thinks of life, what life means to him is also of great importance and may be the bar that shuts out all real health and happiness. The following pages are devoted to certain ideals of life which I would like to give to my patients, the long-time patients who have especially fallen to my lot.

They are not all here, the steps to health and happiness. The reader may even be annoyed and baffled by my indirectness and unwillingness to be specific. That I cannot help—it is a personal peculiarity; I cannot ask any one to live by rule, because I do not believe that rules are binding and final. There must be character behind the rule and then the rule is unnecessary.

All that I have written has doubtless been presented before, in better ways, by wiser men, but I believe that each writer may expect to find his small public, his own particular public who can understand and profit by his teachings, having partly or wholly failed with the others. For that reason I am encouraged to write upon a subject usually shunned by medical men, being assured of at least a small company of friendly readers.

I am grateful to a number of friends and patients who have read the manuscript of the following chapters. These reviewers have been frank and kind and very helpful. I am particularly indebted to Dr. Richard C. Cabot, who has given me much valuable assistance.

I

The Untroubled Mind

Canst thou not minister to a mind diseas'd, pluck from the memory a rooted sorrow, raze out the written troubles of the brain, and with some sweet oblivious antidote cleanse the stuff'd bosom of that perilous stuff which weighs upon the heart?

--*Macbeth.*

When a man tells me he never worries, I am inclined to think that he is either deceiving himself or trying to deceive me. The great roots of worry are conscience, fear, and regret. Undoubtedly we ought to be conscientious and we ought to fear and regret evil. But if it is to be better than an impediment and a harm, our worry must be largely unconscious, and intuitive. The moment we become conscious of worry we are undone. Fortunately, or unfortunately, we cannot leave conscience to its own devices unless our lives are big enough and fine enough to warrant such a course. The remedy for the mental unrest, which is in itself an illness, lies not in an enlightened knowledge of the harmfulness and ineffectiveness of worry, not even in the acquirement of an unconscious conscience, but in the living of a life so full and good that worry cannot find place in it. That idea of worry and conscience, that definition of serenity, simplifies life immensely. To overcome worry by substituting development and growth need never be dull work. To know life in its farther reaches, life in its better applications, is the final remedy—the great undertaking—*it is life*. We must warn ourselves, not infrequently, that the larger life is to be pursued for its own glorious self and not for the sake of peace. Peace may come, a peace so sure that death itself cannot shake it, but we must not expect all our affairs to run smoothly. As a matter of fact they may run badly enough; we shall have our ups and downs, we shall sin and repent, and sin again, but if in the end we live according to our best intuitions, we shall be justified, and we need not worry about the outcome. To put it another way, if we would have the untroubled mind, we must transfer our conscientious efforts from the small details of life—from the worry and fret of common things—into another and a higher atmosphere. We must transfigure common life, dignify it and ennoble it; then, although the old causes of worry may continue, we shall have gained a stature that will make us unconscious masters of the little troubles and in a great degree equal to the larger requirements. Life will be easier, not because we make less effort, but because we are working from another and a better level.

If such a change, and it would be a change for most of us, could come about instantly, in a flash of revelation, that would be ideal, but it would not be life. We must return again and again to the old uninspired state wherein we struggle conscientiously with perverse details. I would not minimize the importance and value of this struggle; only the sooner it changes its level the better for every one concerned. Large serenity must, finally, be earned through the toughening of moral fibre that comes in dealing squarely with perplexing details. Some of this struggle must always be going on, but serener life will come when we begin to concern ourselves with larger factors.

How are we to live the larger life? Partly through uninspired struggle and through the brave meeting of adversity, but partly, also, in a way that may be described as "out of hand," by intuition, by exercise of the quality of mind that sees visions and grasps truths beyond the realms of common thought.

I am more and more impressed with the necessity of inspiration in life if we are to be strong and serene, and so finally escape the pitfalls of worry and conscience. By inspirations I do not mean belief in any system or creed. It is not a stated belief that we need to begin with; that may come in time. We need first to find in life, or at least in nature, an essential beauty that makes its own true, inevitable response within us. We must learn to love life so deeply that we feel its tremendous significance, until we find in the sea and the sky the evidence of an overbrooding spirit too great to be understood, but not too great to satisfy the soul. This is a sort of mother religion—the matrix from which all sects and creeds are born. Its existence in us dignifies us and makes simple, purposeful, and receptive living almost inevitable. We may not know why we are living according to the dictates of our inspiration, but we shall live so and that is the important consideration.

If I urge the acquirement of a religious conception that we may cure the intolerable distress of worry, I do what I have already warned against. It is so easy to make this mistake that I have virtually made it on the same page with my warning. We have no right to seek so great a thing as religious experience that we may be relieved of suffering. Better go on with pain and distress than cheapen religion by making it a remedy. We must seek it for its own sake, or rather, we must not seek it at all, lest, like a dream, it elude us, or change into something else, less holy. Nevertheless, it is true that if we will but look with open, unprejudiced eyes, again and again, upon the sunrise or the stars above us, we shall become conscious of a presence greater and more beautiful than our minds can think. In the experience of that vision strength and peace will come to us unbidden. We shall find our lives raised, as by an unseen force, above the warfare of conscience and worry. We shall begin to know the meaning of serenity and of that priceless, if not wholly to be acquired, possession, the untroubled mind.

I am aware that I shall be misunderstood and perhaps ridiculed by my colleagues when I attempt to discuss religion in any way. Theology is a field in which I have had no training, but that is the very reason why I dare write of it. I do not even assume that there is a God in the traditional sense. The idea is too great to be made concrete and literal. No single fact of nature can be fully understood by our finite minds. But I do feel vaguely that the laws that compass us, and make our lives possible, point always on—"beyond the realms of time and space"—toward the existence of a mighty overruling spirit. If this is a cold and inadequate conception of God, it is at least one that can be held by any man without compromise.

The modern mind is apt to fail of religious understanding and support, because of the arbitrary interpretations of religion which are presented for our acceptance. It is what men say about religion, rather than religion itself, that repels us. Let us think it out for ourselves. If we are open to a simple, even primitive, conception of God, we may still repudiate the creeds and doctrines, but we are likely to become more tolerant of those who find them true and good. We shall be likely in time to find the religion of Christ understandable and acceptable—warm and quick with life. The man who ungrudgingly opens his heart to the God of nature will be religious in the simplest possible sense. He may worry because of the things he cannot altogether understand, and because he falls so far short of the implied ideal.

But he will have enlarged his life so much that the common worries will find little room—he will be too full of the joy of living to spend much conscious thought in worry. Such a man will realize that he cannot afford to spend his time and strength in regretting his past mistakes. There is too much in the future. What he does in the future, not what he has failed to do in the past, will determine the quality of his life. He knows this, and the knowledge sends him into that future with courage and with strength. Finally, in some indefinable way, character will become more important to him than physical health even. Illness is half compensated when a man realizes that it is not what he accomplishes in the world, but what he *is* that really counts, which puts him in touch with the creative forces of God and raises him out of the aimless and ordinary into a life of inspiration and joy.

II

Religio Medici

At all events, it is certain that if any medical man had come to Middlemarch with the reputation of having definite religious views, of being given to prayer and of otherwise showing an active piety, there would have been a general presumption against his medical skill.

--George Eliot.

When a medically educated man talks and writes of religion and of God, he is rightly enough questioned by his brothers—who are too busy with the hard work of practice to be concerned with anything but material problems. To me the word "God" is symbolic of the power which created and which maintains the universe. The sunrise and the stars of heaven give me some idea of his majesty, the warmth and tenderness of human love give me some idea of his divine love. That is all I know, but it is enough to make life glow; it is enough to inspire the most intense devotion to any good cause; it is enough to make me bear suffering with some degree of patience; and it is enough, finally, to give me some confidence and courage even in the face of the great mystery of death. Why this or another conception of God should produce such a profound result upon any one, I do not know, except that in some obscure way it connects the individual with the divine plan, and does not leave him outside in despair and loneliness. However that may be, it will be conceded that a religious conception of some kind does much toward justifying life, toward making it strong and livable, and so has directly to do with certain important problems of illness and health. The most practical medical man will admit that any illness is made lighter and more likely to recover in the presence of hope and serenity in the mind of the patient.

Naturally the great bulk of medical practice calls for no handling other than that of the straight medical sort. A man comes in with a crushed finger, a girl with anæmia—the way is clear. It is only in deeper, more intricate departments of medicine that we altogether fail. The bacteriologist and the pathologist have no use for mental treatment, in their departments. But when we come to the case of the nervously broken-down school teacher, or the worn-out telegrapher, that is another matter. Years may elapse before work can be resumed—years of dependence and anxiety. Here, a new view of life is often more useful than drugs, a view that accepts the situation reasonably after a while, that does not grope blindly and impatiently for a cure, but finds in life an inspiration that makes it good in spite of necessary suffering and limitations. Often enough we cannot promise a cure, but we must be prepared to give something better.

A great deal of the fatigue and unhappiness of the world is due to the fact that we do not go deep enough in our justification for work or play, or for any experience, happy or sad. There is a good deal of a void after we have said, "Art for art's sake," or "Play for the joy of playing," or even after we have said, "I am working for the sake of my family, or for some one who needs my help." That is not enough; and whether we realize it or not, the lack of deeper justification is at the bottom of a restlessness and uncertainty which we might not be willing to acknowledge, but which nevertheless is very real.

I am not satisfied when some moralist says, "Be good and you will be happy." The kind of happiness that comes from a perfunctory goodness is a thing which I cannot understand, and which I certainly do not want. If I work and play and serve and employ, making up the fabric of a busy life, if I attain a very real happiness, I am tormented by the desire to know why I am doing it, and I am not satisfied with the answer I usually get. The patient may not be cured when he is relieved of his anæmia, or when his emaciation has given place to the plumpness and suppleness and physical strength that we call health. The man whom we look upon as well, and who has never known physical illness, is not well in the larger sense until he knows why he is working, why he is living, why he is filling his life with activity. In spite of the elasticity and spring of the world's interests, there must come often, and with a kind of fatal insistence, the deep demand for a cause, for a justification. If there is not an adequate significance behind it, life, with all its courage and accomplishment, seems but a sorry thing, so full of pathos, even in its brightest moments, so shadowed with a sense of loss and of finality that the bravest heart may well fail and the truest courage relax, supported only by the assurance that this way lies happiness or that right is right.

What is this knowledge that the world is seeking, but can never find? What is this final justification? If we seek it in its completeness, we are doomed always to be ill and unsatisfied. If we are willing to look only a little way into the great question, if we are willing to accept a little for the whole, content because it is manifestly part of the final knowledge, and because we know that final knowledge rests with God alone, we shall understand enough to save us from much sorrow and painful incompleteness.

There is, in the infinitely varied and beautiful world of nature, and in the hearts of men, so much of beauty and truth that it is a wonder we do not all realize that these things of common life may be in us and for us the daily and hourly expression of the infinite being we call God. We do not see God, but we do feel and know so much that we may fairly believe to be of God that we do not need to see Him face to face. It is something more than imagination to feel that it is the life of God in our lives, so often unrecognized or ignored, that prompts us to all the greatness and the inspiration and the accomplishment of the world. If we could know more clearly the joy of such a conception, we should dry up at its source much of the unhappiness which is, in a deep and subtle way, at the bottom of many a nervous illness and many a wretched existence.

The happiness which is found in the recognition of kinship with God, through the common things of life, in the experiences which are so significant that they could not spring from a lesser source, the happiness which is not sought, but which is the inevitable result of such recognition—this experience goes a long way toward making life worth living.

If we do have this conception of life, then some of the old, old questions that have vexed so many dwellers upon the earth will no longer be a source of unhappiness or of illness of mind or body. The question of immortality, for instance, which has made us afraid to die, will no longer be a question—we shall not need to answer it, in the presence of God, in our lives and in the world about us. We shall be content finally to accept whatever is in store for us—so it be the will of God. We may even look for something better than mere immortality, something more divine than our gross conception of eternal life.

This is a religion that I believe medical men may teach without hesitation whenever the need shall arise. I know well enough that many a blunt if kindly man cannot bring himself to say these words, even if he believes them, but I do think that in some measure they point the way to what may wisely be taught.

There is a practice of medicine—the common practice—that is concerned with the body only, and with its chemical and mechanical reactions. We can have nothing but respect and admiration for the men who go on year after year in the eager pursuit of this calling. We know that such a work is necessary, that it is just as important as the educational practice of which I write. We know that without the physical side medicine would fail of its usefulness and that disease and death would reap far richer harvests: I only wish the two naturally related aspects of our dealing with patients might not be so completely separated that they lose sight of each other. As a matter of fact, both elements are necessary to our human welfare. If medicine devotes itself altogether to the cure and prevention of physical disease, it will miss half of its possibilities. It is equally true that if we forget the physical necessities in our zeal for spiritual hygiene, we shall get and deserve complete and humiliating failure. Many men will say, "Why mix the two? Why not let the preachers and the philosophers preach and the doctors follow their own ways?" For the most part this may have to be the arrangement, but the doctor who can see and treat the spiritual needs of his patient will always be more likely to cure in the best sense than the doctor who sees only half of the picture. On the other hand, the philosopher is likely to be a comparatively poor doctor, because he knows nothing of medicine, and so can see only the other half of the picture. There is much to be said for the religion of medicine if it can be kept free from cant, if it can be simple and rational enough to be available for the whole world.

❁❁❁

III

Thought and Work

I wish I had a trade! – It would animate my arms and tranquilize my brain.

--Senancour.

"Doe ye nexte thynge." – Old English Proverb.

Since our minds are so constantly filled with anxiety, there would seem to be at least one sure way to be rid of it—to stop thinking.

A great many people believe that the mind will become less effective, that life will become dull and purposeless, unless they are constantly thinking and planning and arranging their affairs. I believe that the mind may easily and wisely be free from conscious thought a good deal of the time, and that the greatest progress and development in mind often comes when the thinker is virtually at rest, when his mind is to all intents and purposes blank. The busy, unconscious mind does its best work in the serenity of an atmosphere which does not interfere and confuse.

It is true that the greatest conceptions do not come to the untrained and undisciplined mind. But do we want great conceptions all the time? There is a technical training for the mind which is, of course, necessary for special accomplishments, but this is quite another matter. Even this kind of thought must not obtrude too much, lest we become conscious of our mental processes and so end in confusion.

One of the greatest benefits of work with the hands, or of objective and constructive work with the mind, is that it saves us from unending hours of thinking. Work should, of course, find its fullest justification as an expression of faith. If we have ever so dim a vision of a greater significance in life, of its close relationship to infinite things, we become thereby conscious of the need of service, of the need of work. It is the easy, natural expression of our faith, the inevitable result of a spiritual contact with the great working forces of the world. It is work above all else that saves us from the disasters of conflicting thought.

A few years ago a young man came to me, suffering from too much thinking. He had just been graduated from college and his head was full of confused ideas and emotions. He was also very tired, having overworked in his preparation for examinations, and because he had not taken the best care of his body. The symptoms he complained of were sleeplessness and worry, together with the inevitable indigestion and headache. Of course, as a physician, I went over the bodily functions carefully, and studied, as far as I might, into the organic conditions. I could find no evidence of physical disease. I did not say, "There is nothing the matter with you"; for the man was sick. I told him that he was tired, that he had thought too much, that he was too much concerned about himself, and that as a result of all this his bodily functions were temporarily upset. He thought he ought to worry about himself, because otherwise he would not be trying to get well. I explained to him that this mistaken obligation was the common reason for worry, and that in this case, at least, it was quite unnecessary and even harmful for him to go on thinking about himself. That helped a little, but not nearly enough, because when a man has overworked, when he has begun to worry, and when his various bodily functions show results of worry, no reasoning, no explanations, can wholly relieve him. I said to this young man, "In spite of your discomforts, in spite of your depression and concern in regard to yourself, you will get well if you will stop thinking about the matter altogether. You must be first convinced that it is best for you to stop thinking, that no harm or violence can result, and then you must be helped in this direction by going to work with your hands—that will be life and progress, it will lead you to health."

Fortunately I had had some experience with nervous illness, and I knew that unless I managed for this man the character and extent of his work, he would not only fail in it, but of its object, and so become more confused and discouraged. I knew the troubled mind, in this instance, might find its solace and its relief in work, but that I must choose the work carefully to suit the individual, and I must see that the nervously fatigued body was not pushed too hard.

In the town where I live is a blacksmith shop, presided over by a genial old man who has been a blacksmith since he was a boy, and in whose hands iron is like clay. I took my patient down to the smithy and said, "Here is a young man whom I want to put to work. He will pay for the chance. I want you first to teach him to make hand-wrought nails." This was a good deal of a joke to the smith and to the patient, but they saw that I was in earnest and agreed to go ahead. We got together the proper tools and proceeded to make nails, a job which is really not very difficult. After an hour's work, I called off my patient, much to his disgust, for he was just beginning to be interested.

But I knew that if he were to keep on until fatigue should come, the whole matter would end in trouble. So the next day, with some new overalls and a leather apron added to the equipment, we proceeded to another hour's work. We went on this way for three or four days, before the time was increased.

The interest of the patient was always fresh, he was eager for more, and he did not taste the dregs of fatigue. Yet he did get the wholesome exercise, and he did get the strong turning of the mind from its worry and concern. Of course, the rest of the day was taken care of in one way or another, but the work was the central feature. In a week, we were at it two hours a day, in three weeks, four hours, and in a month, five hours. He had made a handsome display of hand-wrought nails, a superior line of pokers and shovels for fireplaces, together with a number of very respectable andirons. On each of these larger pieces of handiwork my patient had stamped his initials with a little steel die that was made for him. Each piece was his own, each piece was the product of his own versatility and his own strength. His pride and pleasure in this work were very great, and well they might be, for it is a fine thing to have learned to handle so intractable a material as iron. But in handling the iron patiently and consistently until he could do it without too much conscious thinking, and so without effort, he had also learned to handle himself naturally, more simply and easily.

As a matter of fact, the illness which had brought this boy to me was pretty nearly cured by his blacksmithing, because it was an illness of the mind and of the nerves, and not of the body, although the body had suffered in its turn. That young man, instead of becoming a nervous invalid as he might have done, is now working steadily in partnership with his father, in business in the city. I had found him a very interesting patient, full of originality and not at all the tedious and boresome person he might have been had I listened day after day, week after week to

IV

Idleness

O ye! who have your eyeballs vex'd and tir'd,Feast them upon the wideness of the sea.

--Keats.

Extreme busyness, whether at school or college, kirk or market, is a symptom of deficient vitality; and a faculty for idleness implies a catholic appetite and a strong sense of personal identity.

--Stevenson.

It is an unfortunate fact that very few people are able to be idle successfully. I think it is not so much because we misuse idleness as because we misinterpret it that the long days become increasingly demoralizing. I would ask no one to accept a forced idleness without objection or regret. Such an acceptance would imply a lack of spirit, to say the least. But idleness and rest are not incompatible; neither are idleness and service, nor idleness and contentment. If we can look upon rest as a preparation for service, if we can make it serve us in the opportunity it gives for quiet growth and legitimate enjoyment, then it is fully justified and it may offer advantages and opportunity of the best.

the recital of his ills. I was willing to listen,—I did listen,—but I also gave him a new trend of life, which pretty soon made his complaints sound hollow and then disappear.

Of course, the problem is not always so simple as this, and we must often deal with complexities of body and mind requiring prolonged investigation and treatment. I cite this case because it shows clearly that relief from some forms of nervous illness can come when we stop thinking, when we stop analyzing, and then back up our position with prescribed work.

There may be some nervous invalids who read these lines who will say, "But I have tried so many times to work and have failed." Unfortunately, such failure must often occur unless we can proceed with care and with understanding. But the principle remains true, although it must be modified in an infinite variety to meet the changing conditions of individuals.

I see a great many people who are conscientiously trying to get well from nervous exhaustion. They almost inevitably try too hard. They think and worry too much about it, and so exhaust themselves the more. This is the greater pity because it is the honest and the conscientious people who make the greatest effort. It is very hard for them to realize that they must stop thinking, stop trying, and if possible get to work before they can accomplish their end. We shall have to repeat to them over and over again that they must stop thinking the matter out, because the thing they are attempting to overcome is too subtle to be met in that way. So, if they are fortunate, they may rid themselves of the vagueness and uncertainty of life, until all the multitude of details which go to make up life lose their desultoriness and their lack of meaning, and they may find themselves no longer the subjects of physical or nervous exhaustion.

The chief trouble with idleness is that it so often means introspection, worry, and impatience, especially to those conscientious souls who would fain be about their business.

I have for a long time been accustomed to combat the worry and fret of necessary idleness—not by forbidding it, not by advising struggle and fight against it, but by insisting that the best way to get rid of it is to leave it alone, to accept it. When we do this there may come a kind of fallow time in which the mind enriches and refreshes itself beyond our conception.

I would rather my patient who must rest for a long time would give up all thought of method, would give up all idea of making his mind follow any particular line of thought or absence of thought. I know that the mind which has been under conscious control a good deal of the time is apt to rebel at this freedom and to indulge in all kinds of alarming extravagances. I am sure, however, that the best way to meet these demands for conscious control is to be careless of them, to be willing to experience these extravagances and inconsistencies without fear, in the belief that finally will come a quiet and peace which will be all that we can ask. The peace of mind that is unguided, in the conscious and literal sense, is a thing which too few of us know.

Mr. Arnold Bennett, in his little book, "How to Live on Twenty-four Hours a Day," teaches that we should leave no time unused in our lives; that we should accomplish a great deal more and be infinitely more effective and progressive if we devoted our minds to the definite working-out of necessary problems whenever those times occur in which we are apt to be desultory. I wish here to make a plea for desultoriness and for an idleness which goes even beyond the idleness of the man who reads the newspaper and forgets what he has read. It seems to me better, whether we are sick or well, to allow long periods in our lives when we think only casually. To the good old adage, "Work while you work and play while you play," we might well add, "Rest while you rest," lest in the end you should be unable successfully either to work or play.

A man is not necessarily condemned to tortures of mind because he must rest for a week or a month or a year. I know that there must be anxious times, especially when idleness means dependence, and when it brings hardship to those who need our help. But the invalid must not try constantly to puzzle the matter out. If we do not make ourselves sick with worry, we shall be able sometime to approach active life with sufficient frankness and force. It is the constant effort of the poor, tired mind to solve its problems that not only fails of its object, but plunges the invalid deeper into discouragement and misunderstanding. How cruel this is, and how unfortunate that it should come more commonly to those who try the hardest to overcome their handicaps, to throw off the yoke of idleness and to be well.

When you have tried your best to get back to your work and have failed, when you have done this not once but many times, it is inevitable that misunderstanding should creep in, inevitable that you should question very deeply and doubt not infrequently. Yet the chances are that one of the reasons for your failure is that you have tried too hard, that you have not known how to rest. When you have learned how to rest, when you have learned to put off thinking and planning until the mind becomes fresh and clear, when you are in a fair way to know the joy of idleness and the peace of rest, you are a great deal more likely to get back to efficiency and to find your way along the great paths of activity into the world of life.

It is not so much the idleness, then, as the attempt to overcome its irksomeness, that makes this condition painful. The invalid in bed is in a trap, to be tormented by his thoughts unless he knows the meaning of successful idleness. This knowledge may come to him by such strategy as I have suggested—by giving up the struggle against worry and fret; but peace will come surely, steadily, "with healing in its wings," when the mind is changed altogether, when life becomes free because of a growth and development that finds significance even in idleness, that sees the world with wise and patient eyes.

In a way it does not matter, your physical condition or mine, if our "eyes have seen the glory" that deifies life and makes even its waste places beautiful. What is that view from your window as you lie in your bed? A bit of the sea, if you are fortunate, a corner of garden, surely, the top of an elm tree against the blue. What is it but the revelations of a God in the world? There is enough that is sad and unhappy, but over all are these simple, ineffable things. If the garden is an expression of God in the world, then the world and life are no longer meaningless. Even idleness becomes in some degree bearable because it is a part of a significant world.

Unfortunately, the idleness of disability often means pain, the wear and tear of physical or nervous suffering. That is another matter. We cannot meet it fully with any philosophy. My patients very often beg to know the best way to bear pain, how they may overcome the attacks of "nerves" that are harder to bear than pain. To such a question I can only say that the time to bear pain is before and after. Live in such a way in the times of comparative comfort that the attacks are less likely to appear and easier to bear when they do come. After the pain or the "nervous" attack is over, that is the time to prevent the worst features of another. Forget the distress; live simply and happily in spite of the memory, and you will have done all that the patient himself can do to ward off or to make tolerable the next occasion of suffering. Pain itself—pure physical pain—is a matter for the physician's judgment. It is his business to seek out the causes and apply the remedy.

V

Rules of the Game

It is not growing like a tree in bulk, doth make man better be.

--Ben Jonson.

It is a good thing to have a sound body, better to have a sane mind, but neither is to be compared to that aggregate of virile and decent qualities which we call character.

--Theodore Roosevelt.

The only effective remedy against inexorable necessity is to yield to it.

--Petrarch.

When I go about among my patients, most of them, as it happens, "nervously" sick, I sometimes stop to consider why it is they are ill. I know that some are so because of physical weakness over which they have no control, that some are suffering from the effects of carelessness, some from wilfulness, and more from simple ignorance of the rules of the game. There are so many rules that no one will ever know them all, but it seems that we live in a world of laws, and that if we transgress those laws by ever so little, we must suffer equally, whether our transgression is a mistake or not, and whether we happen to be saints or sinners. There are laws also which have to do with the recovery of poise and balance when these have been lost. These laws are less well observed and understood than those which determine our downfall.

The more gross illnesses, from accident, contagion, and malignancy, we need not consider here, but only those intangible injuries that disable people who are relatively sound in the physical sense. It is true that nervous troubles may cause physical complications and that physical disease very often coexists with nervous illness, but it is better for us now to make an artificial separation. Just what happens in the human economy when a "nervous breakdown" comes, nobody seems to know, but mind and body coöperate to make the patient miserable and helpless. It may be nature's way of holding us up and preventing further injury. The hold-up is severe, usually, and becomes in itself a thing to be managed.

The rules we have wittingly or unwittingly broken are often unknown to us, but they exist in the All-Wise Providence, and we may guess by our own suffering how far we have overstepped them. If a man runs into a door in the dark, we know all about that,—the case is simple,—but if he runs overtime at his office and hastens to be rich with the result of a nervous dyspepsia—that is a mystery. Here is a girl who "came out" last year. She was apparently strong and her mother was ambitious for her social progress. That meant four nights a week for several months at dances and dinners, getting home at 3 a.m. or later. It was gay and delightful while it lasted, but it could not last, and the girl went to pieces suddenly; her back gave out because it was not strong enough to stand the dancing and the long-continued physical strain. The nerves gave out because she did not give her faculties time to rest, and perhaps because of a love affair that supervened. The result was a year of invalidism, and then, because the rules of recovery were not understood, several years more of convalescence. Such common rules should be well enough understood, but they are broken everywhere by the wisest people.

The common case of the broken-down school teacher is more unfortunate. This tragedy and others like it are more often, I believe, due to unwise choice of profession in the first place. The women's colleges are turning out hundreds of young women every year who naturally consider teaching as the field most appropriate and available. Probably only a very small proportion of these girls are strong enough physically or nervously to meet the growing demands of the schools. They may do well for a time, some of them unusually well, for it is the sensitive, high-strung organism that is appreciative and effective. After a while the worry and fret of the requirements and the constant nag of the schoolroom have their effect upon those who are foredoomed to failure in that particular field. The plight of such young women is particularly hard, for they are usually dependent upon their work.

It is, after all, not so much the things we do as the way we do them, and what we think about them, that accomplishes nervous harm. Strangely enough, the sense of effort and the feeling of our own inadequacy damage the nervous system quite as much as the actual physical effort. The attempt to catch up with life and with affairs that go on too fast for us is a frequent and harmful deflection from the rules of the game. Few of us avoid it. Life comes at us and goes by very fast. Tasks multiply and we are inadequate, responsibilities increase before we are ready. They bring fatigue and confusion. We cannot shirk and be true. Having done all you reasonably can, stop, whatever may be the consequences. That is a rule I would enforce if I could. To do more is to drag and fail, so defeating the end of your efforts. If it turns out that you are not fit for the job you have undertaken, give it up and find another, or modify that one until it comes within your capacity. It takes courage to do this—more courage sometimes than is needed to make us stick to the thing we are doing. Rarely, however, will it be necessary for us to give up if we will undertake and consider for the day only such part of our task as we are able to perform. The trouble is that we look at our work or our responsibility all in one piece, and it crushes us. If we cannot arrange our lives so that we may meet their obligations a little at a time, then we must admit failure and try again, on what may seem a lower plane. That is what I consider the brave thing to do. I would honor the factory superintendent, who, finding himself unequal to his position, should choose to work at the bench where he could succeed perfectly.

The habit of uncertainty in thought and action, bred, as it sometimes is, from a lack of faith in man and in God, is, nevertheless, a thing to be dealt with sometimes by itself. Not infrequently it is a petty habit that can be corrected by the exercise of a little will power. I believe it is better to decide wrong a great many times—doing it quickly—than to come to a right decision after weakly vacillating. As a matter of fact, we may trust our decisions to be fair and true if our life's ideals are beautiful and true.

We may improve our indecisions a great deal by mastering their unhappy details, but we shall not finally overcome them until life rings true and until all our acts and thoughts become the solid and inevitable expression of a healthy growing regard for the best in life, a call to right living that is no mean dictum of policy, but which is renewed every morning as the sun comes out of the sea. However inconsequential the habit of indecision may seem, it is really one of the most disabling of bad habits. Its continuance contributes largely to the sum of nervous exhaustion. Whatever its origin, whether it stands in the relation of cause or effect, it is an indulgence that insidiously takes the snap and sparkle out of life and leaves us for the time being colorless and weak.

Next to uncertainty, an uninspired certainty is wrecking to the best of human prospects. The man whose one idea is of making himself and his family materially comfortable, or even rich, may not be coming to nervous prostration, but he is courting a moral prostration that will deny him all the real riches of life and that will in the end reward him with a troubled mind, a great, unsatisfied longing, unless, to be sure, he is too smug and satisfied to long for anything.

The larger life leads us inevitably away from ourselves, away from the super-requirements of our families. It demands of them and of ourselves an unselfishness that is born of a love that finds its expression in the service of God. And what is the service of God if it is not such an entering into the divine purposes and spirit that we become with God re-creators in the world—working factors in the higher evolution of humanity? While we live we shall get and save, we shall use and spend, we shall serve the needs of those dependent upon us, but we shall not line the family nest so softly that our children become powerless. We shall not confine our charities to the specified channels, where our names will be praised and our credit increased. We shall give and serve in secret places with our hearts in our deeds. Then we may possess the untroubled mind, a treasure too rich to be computed. We shall not have it for the seeking; it may exist in the midst of what men may call privations and sorrows; but it will exist in a very large sense and it will be ours. The so-called hard-headed business man who never allows himself to be taken advantage of, whose dealings are always strict and uncompromising, is very apt to be a particularly miserable invalid when he is ill. I cannot argue in favor of business laxity,—I know the imperative need of exactness and finality,—but I do believe that if we are to possess the untroubled mind we must make our lives larger than the field of dollars and cents. The charity that develops in us will make us truly generous and free from the reaction of hardness.

It is a great temptation to go on multiplying the rules of the game. There are so many sensible and necessary pieces of advice which we all need to have emphasized. That is the course we must try to avoid. The child needs to be told, arbitrarily for a while, what is right, and what is wrong, that he must do this, and he must not do that. The time comes, however, when the growing instinct toward right living is the thing to foster—not the details of life which will inevitably take care of themselves if the underlying principle is made right. It must be the ideal of moral teaching to make clear and pure the source of action. Then the stream will be clear and pure. Such a stream will purify itself and neutralize the dangerous inflow along its banks. It is true that great harm may come from the polluted inflows, but they will be less and less harmful as the increasing current from the good source flows down.

We shall have to look well to our habits lest serious ills befall, but that must never be the main concern or we shall find ourselves living very narrow and labored lives; we shall find that we are failing to observe one of the most important rules of the game.

VI

The Nervous Temperament

Beyond the ugly actual, lo, on every side, imagination's limitless domain.

--Browning.

He that too much refines his delicacy will always endanger his quiet.

--Samuel Johnson.

The great refinement of many poetical gentlemen has rendered them practically unfit for the jostling and ugliness of life.

--Stevenson.

It has been my fortune as a physician to deal much with the so-called nervous temperament. I have come both to fear and to love it. It is the essence of all that is bright, imaginative, and fine, but it is as unstable as water. Those who possess it must suffer—it is their lot to feel deeply, and very often to be misunderstood by their more practical friends. All their lives these people will shed tears of joy, and more tears of sorrow. I would like to write of their joy, of the perfect satisfaction, the true happiness that comes in creating new and beautiful things, of the deep pleasure they have in the appreciation of good work in others. But with the instinct of a dog trained for a certain kind of hunting I find myself turning to the misfortunes and the ills.

The very keenness of perception makes painful anything short of perfection. What will such people do in our clanging streets? What of those fine ears tuned to the most exquisite appreciation of sweet sound? What of that refinement of hearing that detects the least departure from the rhythm and pitch in complex orchestral music? And must they bear the crash of steel on stone, the infernal clatter of traffic? Well, yes,—as a matter of fact—they must, at least for a good many years to come, until advancing civilization eliminates the city noise. But it is not always great noises that disturb and distract. There is a story told of a woman who became so sensitive to noise that she had her house made sound-proof: there were thick carpets and softly closing doors; everything was padded. The house was set back from a quiet street, but that street was strewn with tanbark to check the sound of carriages. Surely here was bliss for the sensitive soul. I need not tell the rest of the story, how absolutely necessary noises became intolerable, and the poor woman ended by keeping a man on the place to catch and silence the tree toads and crickets.

There is nothing to excuse the careless and unnecessary noises of the world—we shall dispose of them finally as we are disposing of flamboyant signboards and typhoid flies. But meanwhile, and always, for that matter, the sensitive soul must learn to adjust itself to circumstances and conditions. This adjustment may in itself become a fine art. It is really the art by which the painter excludes the commonplace and irrelevant from his landscape. Sometimes we have to do this consciously; for the most part, it should be a natural, unconscious selection.

I am sure it is unwise to attempt at any time the dulling of the appreciative sense for the sake of peace and comfort. Love and understanding of the beautiful and true is too rare and fine a thing to be lost or diminished under any circumstances. The cure, as I see it, is to be found in the cultivation of the faculty that finds some good in everything and everybody. This is the saving grace—it takes great bulks of the commonplace and distils from the mass a few drops of precious essence; it finds in the unscholarly and the imperfect, rare traces of good; it sees in man, any man, the image of God, to be justified and made evident only in the sublimity of death, perhaps, but usually to be developed in life.

The nervous person is often morose and unsocial—perhaps because he is not understood, perhaps because he falls so short of his own ideals. Often he does not find kindred spirits anywhere. I do not think we should drive such a man into conditions that hurt, but I do believe that if he is truly artistic, and not a snob, he may lead himself into a larger social life without too much sacrifice.

The sensitive, high-strung spirit that does not give of its own best qualities to the world of its acquaintance, that does not express itself in some concrete way, is always in danger of harm. Such a spirit turned in upon itself is a consuming fire. The spirit will burn a long time and suffer much if it does not use its heat to warm and comfort the world of need.

Real illness makes the nervous temperament a much more formidable difficulty —all the sensitive faculties are more sensitive—irritability becomes an obsession and idleness a terror.

The nervous temperament under irritation is very prone to become selfish—and very likely to hide behind this selfishness, calling it temperament. The man who flies into a passion when he is disturbed, or who spends his days in torment from the noises of the street; the woman of high attainment who has retired into herself, who is moody and unresponsive,—these unfortunates have virtually built a wall about their lives, a wall which shuts out the world of life and happiness. From the walls of this prison the sounds of discord and annoyance are thrown back upon the prisoner intensified and multiplied. The wall is real enough in its effect, but will cease to exist when the prisoner begins to go outside, when he begins to realize his selfishness and his mistake. Then the noises and the irritations will be lost in the wider world that is open to him. After all, it is only through unselfish service in the world of men that this broadening can come.

There is no lack of opportunity for service. Perhaps the simplest and most available form of service is charity,—the big, professional kind, of course, —and beyond that the greater field of intimate and personal charity. I know a girl of talent and ability—herself a nervous invalid—sick and helpless for the lack of a little money which would give her a chance to get well. I do not mean money for luxuries, for foolish indulgences, but money to buy opportunity—money that would lift her out of the heavy morass of poverty and give her a chance. She falls outside the beaten path of charity. She is not reached by the usual philanthropies. I also know plenty of people who could help that girl without great sacrifice. They will not do it because they give money to the regular charities—they will not do it because sometimes generosity has been abused. So they miss the chance of broadening and developing their own lives.

I know well enough that objective interest can rarely be forced—it must usually come the other way about—through the broadening of life which makes it inevitable. Sometimes I wish I could force that kind of development, that kind of charity. Sometimes I long to take the rich neurasthenic and make him help his brother, make him develop a new art that shall save people from sorrow and loss. We are all together in this world, and all kin; to recognize it and to serve the needs of the unfortunate as we would serve our own children is the remedy for many ills. It is the new art, the final and greatest of all artistic achievements; it warms our hearts and opens our lives to all that is wholesome and good. This is one of the crises in which my theory of "inspiration first" may fail. Here the charity may have to come first, may have to be insisted upon before there can be any inspiration or any further joy in life. It is not always charity in the usual sense that is required; sometimes the charity that gives something besides money is best. But charity in any good sense means self-forgetfulness, and that is a long way on the road to nervous health. Give of yourself, give of your substance, and you will cease to be troubled with the penalties of selfishness. Then take the next step—that gives not because life has come back, but because the world has become larger and warmer and happier. When the giver gives of his sympathy and of his means because he wants to,—not because he has to do so,—he will begin to know what I mean when I say it is better to have the inspiration first.

VII

Self-Control

He only earns his freedom and existence who daily conquers them anew.

--Goethe.

A good many writers on self-control and kindred subjects insist that we shall conscientiously and consciously govern our mental lives. They say, "You must get up in the morning with determination to be cheerful." They insist that in spite of annoyance or trouble you shall keep a smiling face, and affirm to yourself over and over again the denial of annoyance.

I do not like this kind of self-control. I wish I could admire it and approve it, but I find I cannot because it seems to me self-conscious and superficial. It is better than nothing and unquestionably adds greatly to the sum of human happiness. But I do not think we ought to be cheerful if we are consumed with trouble and sorrow. The fact is we ought not to be for long beyond a natural cheerfulness that comes from the deepest possible sources. While we are sad, let us be so, simply and naturally; but we must pray that the light may come to us in our sorrow, that we may be able soon and naturally to put aside the signs of mourning.

The person who thinks little of his own attitude of mind is more likely to be well controlled and to radiate happiness than one who must continually prompt himself to worthy thoughts. The man whose heart is great with understanding of the sorrow and pathos of life is far more apt to be brave and fine in his own trouble than one who must look to a motto or a formula for consolation and advice. Deep in the lives of those who permanently triumph over sorrow there is an abiding peace and joy. Such peace cannot come even from ample experience in the material world. Despair comes from that experience sometimes, unless the heart is open to the vital spirit that lies beyond all material things, that creates and renews life and that makes it indescribably beautiful and significant. Experience of material things is only the beginning. In it and through it we may have experience of the wider life that surrounds the material.

Our hearts must be opened to the courage that comes unbidden when we feel ourselves to be working, growing parts of the universe of God. Then we shall have no more sorrow and no more joy in the pitiful sense of the earth, but rather an exaltation which shall make us masters of these and of ourselves. We shall have a sympathy and charity that shall need no promptings, but that flow from us spontaneously into the world of suffering and need.

Beethoven was of a sour temper, according to all accounts, but he wrote his symphonies in the midst of tribulations under which few men would have worked at all. When we have felt something of the spirit that makes work inevitable, it will be as though we had heard the eternal harmonies. We shall write our symphonies, build our bridges, or do our lesser tasks with dauntless purpose, even though the possessions that men count dear are taken from us. Suppose we can do very little because of some infirmity: if that little has in it the larger inspiration, it will be enough to make life full and fine. The joy of a wider life is not obtainable in its completeness; it is only through a lifetime of service and experience that we can approach it. That is the proof of its divine origin—its unattainableness. "God keep you from the she wolf and from your heart's deepest desire," is an old saying of the Rumanians. If we fully obtain our desires, we prove their unworthiness. Does any one suppose that Beethoven attained his whole heart's desire in his music? He might have done so had he been a lesser man. He was not a cheerful companion. That is unfortunate, and shows that he failed in complete inspiration and in the ordinary kind of self-control. He was at least sincere, and that helped not a little to make him what he was. I would almost rather a man would be morose and sincere than cheerful from a sense of duty.

Our knowledge of the greater things of life must always be substantiated and worked out into realities of service, or else we shall be weak and ineffective. The charity that balks at giving, reacts upon a man and deadens him. I am always insisting that we must not live and serve through a sense of duty, but that we must find the inspiration first. It is better to give ourselves to service not for the sake of finding God, but because we have found Him and because our souls have grown in the finding until we cannot help giving. If we have grown to such a stature we shall be able to meet sorrow and loss bravely and simply. We shall feel for ourselves and for others in their troubles as Forbes Robertson did when he wrote to his friend who had met with a great loss: "I pray that you may never, never, never get over this sorrow, but through it, into it, into the very heart of God." All this is very unworldly, no doubt, and yet I will venture the assertion that such a standard and such a method will come nearer to the mark of successful and well-controlled living than the most carefully planned campaign of duty. If we plan to make life fine, if we say, in effect, "I will be good and cheerful, no matter what happens," we are beginning at the wrong end. We may be able to work back from our mottoes to real living, but the chances are we shall stop somewhere by the way, too confused and uncertain to go on. Self-control, at its best, is not a conscious thing. It is not well that we should try to be good, but that we should so dignify our lives with the spirit of good that evil becomes well-nigh impossible to us.

VIII

The Lighter Touch

Heart not so heavy as mine, wending late home, as it passed my window whistled itself a tune.

--Emily Dickinson.

I have never seen good come from frightening worriers. It is no doubt wise to speak the truth, but it seems to me a mistake to say in public print or in private advice that worry leads to tragedies of the worst sort. No matter how hopeful we may be in our later teaching about the possibilities of overcoming worry, the really serious worrier will pounce upon the original tragic statement and apply it with terrible insistence to his own case.

I would not minimize the seriousness of worry, but I am convinced that we can rarely overcome it by direct voluntary effort. It does not go until we forget it, and we do not forget it if we are always trying consciously to overcome it. We worriers must go about our business—other business than that of worry.

Life is serious—alas, too serious—and full enough of pathos. We cannot joke about its troubles; they are real. But, at least, we need not magnify them. Why should we act as though everything depended upon our efforts, even the changing seasons and the blowing winds? No doubt we are responsible for our own acts and thoughts and for the welfare of those who depend upon us. The trouble is we take unnecessary responsibilities so seriously that we overreach ourselves and defeat our own good ends.

I would make my little world more blessedly careless—with an *abandon* that loves life too much to spoil it with worry. I would cherish so great a desire for my child's good that I could not scold and bear down upon him for every little fault, making him a worrier too, but, instead, I would guide him along the right path with pleasant words and brave encouragement. The condemnation of faults is rarely constructive.

We had better say to the worriers, "Here is life; no matter what unfortunate things you may have said or done, you must put all evil behind you and live—simply, bravely, well." The greater the evil, the greater the need of forgetting. Not flippantly, but reverently, leave your misdeeds in a limbo where they may not rise to haunt you. This great thing you may do, not with the idea of evading or escaping consequences, but so that past evil may be turned into present and future good. The criminal himself is coming to be treated this way. He is no longer eternally reminded of his crime. He is taken out into the sunshine and air and is given a shovel to dig with. A wonderful thing is that shovel. With it he may bury the past and raise up a happier, better future. We must care so much to expiate our sins that we are willing to neglect them and live righteously. That is true repentance, constructive repentance.

We cannot suddenly change our mental outlook and become happy when grief has borne us down. "For the broken heart silence and shade,"—that is fair and right. I would say to those who are unhappy, "Do not try to be happy, you cannot force it; but let peace come to you out of the great world of beauty that calmly surrounds our human suffering, and that speaks to us quietly of God." Genuine laughter is not forced, but we may let it come back into our lives if we know that it is right for it to come.

We have all about us instances of the effectiveness of the lighter touch as applied to serious matters. The life of the busy surgeon is a good example. He may be, and usually is, brimming with sympathy, but if he were to feel too deeply for all his patients, he would soon fail and die. He goes about his work. He puts through a half-dozen operations in a way that would send cold shivers down the back of the uninitiated. And yet he is accurate and sure as a machine. If he were to take each case upon his mind in a heavy, consequential way, if he were to give deep concern to each ligature he ties, and if he were to be constantly afraid of causing pain, he would be a poor surgeon. His work, instead of being clean and sharp, would suffer from over-conscientiousness. He might never finish an operation for fear his patient would bleed to death. Such a man may be the reverse of flippant, and yet he may actually enjoy his somber work. Cruel, bloodthirsty? Not at all. These men—the great surgeons—are as tender as children. But they love their work, they really care very deeply for their patients. The successful ones have the lighter touch and they have no time for worry.

Sometimes we wish to arouse the public conscience. Do the long columns of figures, the impressive statistics, wake men to activity? It is rather the keen, bright thrust of the satirist that saves the day. Once in a New England town meeting there was a movement for a much-needed new schoolhouse. By the installation of skylights in the attic the old building had been made to accommodate the overflow of pupils. The serious speakers in favor of the new building had left the audience cold, when a young man arose and said he had been up into the attic and had seen the wonderful skylights that were supposed to meet the needs of the children. "I have seen them," he said; "we used to call them scuttles when I was a boy." A hundred thousand dollars was voted for the new schoolhouse.

There is a natural gayety in most of us which helps more than we realize to keep us sound. The pity is that when responsibilities come and hardships come, we repress our lighter selves sternly, as though such repression were a duty. Better let us guard the springs of happiness very, very jealously. The whistling boy in the dark street does more than cheer himself on the way. He actually protects himself from evil, and brings courage not only to himself, but to those who hear him. I do not hold for false cheerfulness that is sometimes affected, but a brave show of courage in a forlorn hope will sometimes win the day. It is infinitely more likely to win than a too serious realization of the danger of defeat. The show of courage is often not a pretense at all, but victory itself.

The need of the world is very great and its human destiny is in our hands. Half of those who could help to right the wrongs are asleep or too selfishly immersed in their own affairs. We need more helpers like my friend of the skylights. Most of us are far too serious. The slumberers will slumber on, and the worriers will worry, the serious people will go ponderously about until some one shows them how ridiculous they are and how pitiful.

❁❁❁

IX

Regrets and Forebodings

Regret avails little – still less remorse – the one keeps alive the old offense, the other creates new offenses.

--Goethe.

The unrepentant sinner walks abroad. Unfortunately for us moralists he seems to be having a very good time. We must not condone him, though he may be a very lovable person; neither must we altogether condemn him, for he may be repentant in the very best way of all ways, the way that forgets much and leaves behind more, because life is so fine that it must not be spoiled, and because progress is in every way better than retrospection. The fact is, that repentance is too often the fear of punishment, and such fear is, to say the least, unmanly. I would rather be a lovable sinner than one of the people who repent because they cannot bear to think of the consequences. Knowledge and fear of consequences undoubtedly keep a great many young people from the so-called sins of ignorance. But there must be something behind knowledge and fear of consequences to stop the youth of spirit from doing what he is inclined to do. Over and over again we must go back to the appreciation of life's dignity and beauty—to the consciousness of the spirit of God behind and in the world if we are to find a balance and a character that will "deliver us from evil."

When we have found this consciousness—when we live it and breathe it, we shall be far less apt to sin, and when we have sinned, as we all must in the course of our blundering lives, we shall not waste our time in regret or in the fear of consequences. If the God we dream of is as great as the sea, or as beautiful as a tree, we need not fear Him. He will be tender, and just at the same time. He will be as forgiving as He is strong. The best we can do, then, is to leave our sins in the hand of God and go our way, sadder and wiser, maybe, but not regretting too much, not fearing any more.

There is a new idea in medicine—the development of which has been one of the most striking achievements of modern times—the idea of psychanalysis as taught and advocated by Freud in Germany. The plan is to study the subconscious mind of the nervous patient by means of hypnotism, to assist the patient to recall all the mental experiences of his past,—even his very early childhood,—and in this way to make clear the origin of the misconceptions and the unfortunate impressions which have presumably exerted their influence through the years. The new system includes, also, the interpretation of dreams, their effect upon the conscious life and their influence upon the mentality. Very wonderful results are reported from the pursuit of this method. Many a badly warped and twisted life has been straightened out and renewed when the searchlight has revealed the hidden influences that have been at work and which have made trouble. The repression of conscious or unconscious feelings can no doubt change the whole mental life. We should have the greatest respect for the men who are doing this work. It requires, I am told, an almost unbelievable amount of patience and time to accomplish the analysis. No doubt the adult judgment of childish follies is a direct means of disposing of their harmful influence in life, the surest way of losing the conscious or unconscious regrets that sadden many lives. There are probably many cases of disturbed and troubled mind that can be cured in this way only. The method does not appeal to me because I am so strongly inclined to take people as they are, to urge a forgetfulness that does not really forget, but which goes on bravely to the development of life. This development cannot proceed without the understanding that life may be made so beautiful that sins and failures are lost in progress. Some of us may need the subtle analysis of our lives to make clear the points where we went astray in our thoughts and ideas, but many of us, fortunately, are able to take ourselves for better or for worse, sins and all. Most of us ought to do that, for the most part, if we are to progress and live. Sometimes the revelations of evils we know not of result in complications rather than simplification, as in the case of a boy who wrote to me and said that since he had learned of his early sins he had made sure that he could never be well. Instead of going into further analysis with him, I assured him that, while it was undoubtedly his duty to regret all the evil of his life, it was a still greater duty to go on and live the rest of it well, and that he could do so if he would open his eyes to the possibilities of unselfish service.

I am very much inclined to preach against self-analysis and the almost inevitable regret and despair that accompany it.

One of my patients decided some time ago that her life was wasted, that she had accomplished nothing. It was true that she had not the endurance to meet the usual demands of social or even family life, and that for long periods she had to give up altogether. But it happened that she had the gift of musical understanding, that she had studied hard in younger days. With a little urging the gift was made to grow again and to serve not only the patient's own needs, but to bring very great pleasure to every one who listened to her playing. That rare, true ability was worth everything, and she came to realize it in time. The gift of musical expression is a very great thing, and I succeeded in making this woman understand that she should be happy in that ability even if nothing else should be possible.

Often enough nothing that can compare with music exists, and life seems wholly barren. Rather cold comfort it seems at first to assure a person who is helpless that character is the greatest thing in the world, but that is the final truth. The most limited and helpless life may glow with it and be richer than imagination can believe. It is never time to regret—and never time to despair. The less analysis the better. When it comes to character, live, grow, and get a deeper and deeper understanding of life—of life that is near to God and so capable of wrong only as we turn away from Him. "Do not say things; what you are stands over you and thunders so, I cannot hear what you say to the contrary." We shall do well not to forget that, whatever failures or mistakes we have made, there is infinite possibility ahead of us, that character is the greatest thing in the world, and that most good character has been built upon mistakes and failures. I believe there is no sin which may not make up the fabric of its own forgiveness in the living of a free, self-sacrificing life. I know of no bodily ill nor handicap which we may not eventually rise above and beyond by means of brave spiritual progress. The body may fail us, but the spirit reaches on and into the great world of God.

X

The Virtues

The virtues hide their vanquished fires within that whiter flame –
till conscience grows irrelevant and duty but a name.

--Frederick Lawrence Knowles.

In most books I have read on "nerves" and similar subjects, advice is given, encouragement is given, but the necessity for patience is not made clear. Patience is typical of all the other virtues. Many a man has followed the best of advice for a time, and has become discouraged because the promised results did not materialize. It is disappointing, surely, to have lived upon a diet for months only to find that you still have dyspepsia, or to have followed certain rules of morality with great precision and enthusiasm without obtaining the untroubled mind. We are accustomed to see results in the material world and naturally expect them everywhere. The trouble is we do not always recognize improvements when we see them, and we insist upon certain preconceived changes as a result of our endeavors. The physician is apt rashly to promise definite physical accomplishments in a given time. He is courting disappointment and distrust when he does so. We all want to get relief from our symptoms, and we are inclined to insist upon a particular kind of relief so strongly that we fail to appreciate the possibilities of another and a better relief which may be at hand. The going astray in this particular is sometimes very unfortunate. I have known a man to rush frantically from one doctor to another, trying to obtain relief for a particular pain or discomfort, unwilling to rest long enough to find out that the trouble would have disappeared naturally if he had taken the advice of the first physician, to live without impatience and within his limitations.

The human body is a very complex organism, and sometimes pain and distress are better not relieved, since they may be the expression of some deeper maladjustment which must first be straightened out. This is also true of the mind—in which the unhappy proddings of conscience had better not be cured by anodynes or by evasion unless we are prepared to go deeply enough to make them disappear spontaneously. We must sometimes insist upon patience, though it should exist as a matter of course—patience with ourselves and with others. The physician who demands and secures the greatest degree of patience from his clients is the most successful practitioner, for no life can go on successfully without patience. If patience can be spontaneous,—the natural result of a broadening outlook,—then it will be permanent and serviceable; the other kind, that exists by extreme effort, may do for a while, but it is a poor makeshift.

I always feel like apologizing when I ask a man or a woman to be tolerant or charitable or generous or, for that matter, to practice any of the ordinary virtues. Sound living should spring unbidden from the very joy of life; it should need no justification and certainly no urging. But unfortunately, as the world now stands, there are men and groups of men who do not see the light. There is a wide contagion of selfishness and short-sightedness among the well-to-do, and a necessary federation of protection and selfishness among the poor. The practical needs of life, artificial as they are among the rich, and terribly insistent as they are among the poor, blind us to larger considerations.

If all matters of welfare, public or private, could be treated unselfishly, how quickly we should be rid of some of the great evils that afflict the race. I am inclined to think that much of the goodness of people does come in that way, unconsciously, naturally, as the light flows from the sun. Yet I suppose that in our present order, and until, through the years, the better time arrives, we must very often ask ourselves and others to be good and to be charitable, just because it is right, or worse still because it is good policy.

A man grows better, more human, more intelligent, as he practices the virtues. He is safer, no doubt, and the world is better. It is even true that, by the constant practice of virtues, he may come finally to espouse goodness and become thoroughly good. That is the hopeful thing about it and the reason why we may consistently ask or demand the routine practice of the virtues. But let us hold up all the time in our teaching and in our lives the other course, the development of the inspiration that includes all virtues and that makes all our way easy and plain in a world where confusion reigns, because men are going at the problem of right living the wrong way around.

The practice of good living will never be easy in its details, but if it is sure in its inspiration there will be no question of the final triumph. We shall have to fight blindly sometimes and with all the strength and persistence of animals at bay. We shall fail sometimes, too, and that is not always the worst thing that can happen. It is the glory of life that we shall slowly triumph over ourselves and the world. It is the glory of life that out of sore trouble, in the midst of poverty and human injustice, may rise, spontaneous and serene, the spirit of self-sacrifice, the unconquerable spirit of service that does not question, that expresses the divine tenderness in terms of human love. Through the times of darkness and doubt which must inevitably come, there will be for those who cherish such a vision, and who come back to it again and again, no utter darkness, no trouble that wholly crushes, no loss that wholly destroys.

If we could not understand it before, it will slowly dawn upon us that the life of Christ exemplified all these things. Charity, kindliness, service, patience,—all these things which have seemed so hard will become in our lives, as in his, the substance and expression of our faith. The great human virtues will become easy and natural, the untroubled mind, or as much of it as is good to possess, will be ours, not because we have escaped trouble, but because we have disarmed it, have welcomed it even, so long as it has served to strengthen and ennoble our lives.

XI

The Cure by Faith

The healing of his seamless dress is by our beds of pain – we touch Him in life's throng and press, and we are whole again.

--Whittier.

I cannot finish my little book of ideals without writing some things that are in my mind about cure by faith or by prayer. It is a subject that I approach with hesitation because of the danger of misunderstanding. No subject is more difficult and none is more important for the invalid to understand. We hear a great deal about the wonderful cures of Christian Science or of similar agencies, and we all know of people who have been restored to usefulness by such means. Has the healing of Christ again become possible on earth? No one would be more eager to accept it and acknowledge it than the physician if it were really so. But careful investigation always reveals the fact that the wonderful cures are not of the body but of the mind. It is easy enough to say that a cancer or tuberculosis has been cured by faith, and apparently easy for many people to believe it, but alas, the proof is wanting. The Christian Scientist, honest and sincere as he may be, is not qualified to say what is true disease and what is not. What looks like diseased tissue recovers, but medical men know that it could not have been diseased in the most serious sense, and that the prayer for recovery could have had nothing to do with the cure, save in a very indirect way.

The man who discards medicine for philosophy or religion is courting unnecessary suffering and even death. The worst part of it is that he may induce some one else to make the same mistake with similar results. In writing this opinion I am in no way denying the great significance and value of faith nor of the prayerful and trustful mind. If it cannot cure actual physical disease, faith can accomplish veritable miracles of healing in the mind of the patient. No thoughtful or honest medical man will deny it. Nor will most medical men deny that the course of almost any physical illness may be modified by faith and prayer. I am almost saying that there is no known medicine of such potency. Every bodily function is the better for the conquering spirit that transcends the earth and finds its necessary expression in prayer.

There really need be no issue or disagreement between medicine and faith cure. At its best, one is not more wonderful than the other, and both aim to accomplish the same end—the relief of human suffering. When the two are merged, as some day they will be, we shall be surprised to discover how alike they are. Christian Science is rightly scorned by medical men because it is unscientific, because it makes absurd and untenable claims outside its own field, and because it has not as yet investigated that field in the scientific spirit. When proper study and investigation have been made it will be found that faith cure, not in its present state, but in some future development, will have an immense field of usefulness. It will be worthy of as much respect in that field as medicine proper in its own sphere. As a matter of fact both medicine and faith cure are miraculous in a very real sense, as both depend for efficiency now and always upon the same great laws which may be fairly called divine. What is the discovery that the serum of a horse will under certain circumstances cure diphtheria? Does it not mean that man is tapping sources of power far beyond his understanding? Is man responsible save as the agent? Did he produce the complex animal chemistry that makes this cure possible? Did man make the horse, or the laws that control the physiology and pathology of that animal? Here, then, is faith cure in its largest and best sense. The biologist may not be willing to admit it, but his faith in these great laws of God have made possible the cure of a dread disease. Here, as in all matters of pure religion, it is what men say and write, not the fact itself, that makes all the misunderstanding; we make our judgments and conceive our prejudices from mere surface considerations. Call life what you will,—leave out the symbolic word "God" altogether,—the facts remain. The true scientific spirit must reverence and adore the power that lies behind creation. It is as inconsistent for the bacteriologist to be an unbeliever as it is for the Christian Scientist to deny the value of bacteriology. Medicine is infinitely farther advanced than Christian Science, and yet Christian Science has grasped some truth that the natural scientist has stupidly missed. When an obsession is thrown off and courage substituted for fear, we witness as important a "cure" as can be shown to the credit of surgery. If the Christian Scientists and the other faith-curers were only less superficial and less narrow in their explanation of the facts, if they would condescend to study the diseases they treat, they would be entitled to, and would receive, more respect and consideration.

The cure and prevention of disease through the agency of man are evidently part of the divine plan. Our eagerness to advance along the lines of investigation and practice is but that divine plan in action. The truly scientific spirit will neglect no possible curative agent. When scientific men ridicule prayer, they are thinking not of the real thing which is above all possible criticism, but of the feeble and often pathetic groping for the real thing. We ask in our prayers for impossible blessings that would invert the laws of God and change the face of nature—very well, we must be prepared for disappointment. The attitude of prayer may, indeed, transform our own lives and make possible for us experiences that would otherwise have been impossible. But our pathetic demands—we shall never know how forlorn and weak they are. Prayer is the opening of the heart to the being we call God—it is most natural and reasonable. If we pray in our weakness and blindness for what we may not have, there is, nevertheless, a wonderful re-creative effect within us. The comfort and peace of such communion is beyond all else healing and restoring in its influence upon the troubled and anxious mind of man. The poet or the scientist who bows in adoration before the glory of God revealed in nature, prays in effect to that God and his soul is refreshed and renewed. The poor wretch who stands blindfolded before the firing squad, waiting the word that ends the life of a military spy, is near enough to God—and the whispered prayer upon his lips is cure for the wounds that take his life.

The best kind of prayer seeks not and asks not for physical relief or benefit, but opens the heart to its maker, and so receives the cure of peace that is a greater miracle than any yet wrought by man. Under the influence of that cure the sick are well and the dead are alive again. With the courage and spirit of such a cure in our lives, we shall inevitably do our utmost to relieve, by any good means, the physical suffering of the world. We shall follow the laws of nature. We shall study them with the utmost care. We shall take nothing for granted, since by less careful steps we shall miss the divine law and so go astray. The science of healing will become no chance and irrational thing. We shall use all the natural means to relieve and prevent suffering—there will be no scoring of one set of doctors by another because all will have one purpose. But more to the point than that, men will discover that health in its largest sense consists in living devout and prayerful lives whereunto shall be revealed in good time all that our finite minds can know and use. There will be no suffering of the body in the old and pitiful sense, for we shall be so much alive that disease and death can no longer claim us.

www.ingramcontent.com/pod-product-compliance
Lightning Source LLC
LaVergne TN
LVHW100734061126
851857LV00011B/528
* 9 7 8 9 3 5 9 5 7 6 9 4 7 *